This story is not one that I knew I ever wanted to tell. I have gotten used to living with a secret. Having a locked door that I never open. I have gotten used to carrying an added weight, accustomed to the darkness that didn't use to be inside me. I have grown used to hiding things, myself included.

There is a part of me that is locked away behind that door; the one that I never open. Only I know about her, the girl that resides there. I have never introduced her to anyone. She is a feral thing. Not yet five years old. She is made of everything raw and shattered glass. She is not beautiful or pretty or nice. She is pain and suffering and nightmares and fury and loss and screams in the middle of the night.

I have been quite positive that you would not like her. I do not like her myself. In fact, I have hated her. Despised her. I have been so ashamed of the creature that lives behind the locked door that I resolved quite firmly that you never discover her existence. This creature, this part of me, has not been allowed to speak. I have kept her silent. Her words fall like knives and she does not know how to soften them. She does not know how to make any of what she wants to say, what she has to say, less ugly. How do you tell a horror story to the ones you love without leaving them horrified? I swore never to let her out. Never to let her wreak her damage, unleash her madness on my world the way she had on my own heart.

But nothing comes without a consequence. And when I locked her away, she took something with her of mine. She took my voice. My words. They have been with her, suppressed under lock and key for nearly five years. The story of what happened. Impossible to tell.

And now, increasingly, ever more, impossible not to tell.

You see, I have to let her out.

I have already had something stolen from me.

She knows this.

It is her leverage; that maybe this is the sole thing that I might find unbearable.

You see, when you are robbed of something, something that is irreplaceable, something you never wanted to give, something you can never get back, what you have left becomes that much more precious. You become conscious of it in a way that you were not before. It becomes insupportable, the idea that something else be taken away from you. Insupportable that you not only be robbed, but that the words to tell the story of that crime would be stolen too.

And so, I'm letting her out. She will undoubtedly tear into your flesh as you turn these pages and burn your fingertips as they skim over these words. She will be unapologetic, and it will seem cruel. Forgive her. Try to understand her. Grief is not kind. Anguish is not gentle. And as dark and as heavy and as horrific as these words are – they are mine.

And I'm taking them back.

January 17th 2015

It happens in the dead of winter. It happens in a nothing town, sometime after midnight. Tree branches hang naked, lifeless above a frozen ground. The world is numb. Dark. Everything is silent. Snowflakes fall. In the morning, no one will notice they are new. That something is different. No one will notice anything at all.

A girl is murdered. She is naked, lifeless, hanging above her frozen body, watching, numb, silent as it happens. When it is over, she falls back inside of herself. In the morning, no one will notice that she is different. Dark. No one will notice anything at all.

Standing in front of the bathroom mirror, she stares at her reflection. It is missing. It's not that she can't see her face in the sense that her vision is blurred or obstructed, it's that, quite plainly, with horrific clarity, where her face should be, there is nothing. It simply isn't there at all. It's an odd thing. Seeing an absence. A nothingness. Her face. Gone. All she sees is her body and this confirms what she already knows. She died last night. All that mattered then, all that remains now, is her body. She was murdered. Wherever souls go, hers has gone. She is a ghost.

The only thing more astonishing than this is that somehow, impossibly, she still exists. Despite the fact that she was banished from her body, ruthlessly ejected to watch her own murder from above her bed, she is stubbornly, obstinately, nauseatingly, still there. Despite the fact that her body froze, betrayed her, it is still traitorously beating, breathing. There is none of the peace that comes with closed coffins. She is still there. But there is an emptiness rattling around inside of her. She is hollow.

From the top of a white paper topped table, her legs dangle off into nothingness, oblivion. She flinches away from hands that try to touch her. She refuses to take off her clothes. Clinical voices swirl around the room and they sound nearly as cold as she feels, and she hears none of them and all of them at once. She is a statistic. White coats come and go. The lab nurse enters with test results. *"No STDs. You're clean. Anything else I can do for you? Maybe just some condoms?"* The nurse smiles. The concept of a smile feels so foreign to her that it makes the woman appear strangely grotesque, alien. It is so very clear that no one informed the lab nurse, that there is a break somewhere in their meticulous medical chain, that the nurse is unaware of why, of how she ended up there, legs dangling off the top of the white paper topped table. The offer rings in her head, echoing in all of the empty spaces, filling up the cavernous void inside of her bones. *"Maybe just some condoms?"* Somewhere below the depths of icy numbness, she is vaguely aware of a coiling rage, a heavy, dull fury. She wants to fling the truth back at her, watch it as it hits the woman in the face and sinks into her chest, watch with satisfaction as the smile disappears, watch her realize. She wants her to hurt. She wants her to hurt like she is hurting. Her eyes narrow.

She knows what she is thinking behind the smile. Slut. Too many nights of wild sex. She wants her to know the way he ripped her open. The way he tore her apart. The way he didn't care, didn't stop. She wants to scream at her that she was a virgin. She stares at the woman blankly. She doesn't answer. There are no words. She says nothing, and walks past her, out of the room. The fury settles itself amongst the ice.

She is curled up in her childhood bed, banished forever from her own childhood. Immobile. She listens to her breath, feels her chest rise and fall. Every continuous inhale and exhale astonish her. All of her words catch, frozen in her throat when her mother discovers her lying there. Home from college for the weekend. Unexpected. Unannounced. She is supposed to say something, anything. She is supposed to explain. How is she supposed to explain this? That's she's dead, that she was murdered, that she saw it all happen, her soul discarded, her body torn open, broken apart. She wants to be held, she wants to be warm again, she wants to be put back together. Bandaged up, like she's eleven and just fallen off her bike, scraped her knee. Her mother guesses at different versions of that midnight. She is incoherent, incapable of offering anything but a weak nod when she gets close. She cannot say the word. *Rape.* She sees the despairing confusion in her mother's eyes, and she has no answers to any of her questions. *"Did you say no? But darling how was the poor boy to know?"* She cannot bear to tell her father. Her mother relays the message, tells the story of the midnight she does not understand, and her father holds her, tells her that it could have been so much worse. She stands in his arms, wills her breathing to slow. This is nothing she tells herself. This is nothing. Nothing. Nothing. Nothing. *Nothing.*

She goes back to school. Tells no one else. She rearranges all of her furniture at 3 am, so that maybe, when she closes her eyes at night, when she lays down to sleep in that same bed, maybe she won't see him. Maybe she won't feel him.

Headlights of passing cars blur together in the frosted window shield. She stares ahead, unblinking, as the road, the miles disappear beneath her. She thinks in a reflective, detached manner, how simple, how easy it would be to simply drift into the lane of oncoming traffic. A little pressure on the wheel. That's all it would take. She goes on lots of long drives like this. The area surrounding the nothing town is littered with mansions from the Gilded age. Houses that were never homes from an era built on illusion. She parks the car in front of an estate frozen in time amid the snow-covered hills. She sits there for hours, just looking at it. It has never been more obvious to her: marble and stone are beautiful, but so cold. The mansion is a hollow shell. She finds comfort in the fact that her body is not the only façade to fool the world to the emptiness, the frigidity of its interior. It doesn't escape her attention that despite this, so many years later, the walls of the old house are still standing. When she drives back that night, back to the bedroom, back to the bed where he murdered her, she is still watching the cars in the other lane, but she is made of stone, like the mansion walls. Her hand never slips from the wheel.

She no longer wants to go out dancing, to parties. She thinks if she ever runs across that smell again – stale beer and sweat and agony- she will fall apart. Weeks and then months of Friday and Saturday nights go by; her friends become impatient. Eventually they stop asking if she wants to go with them. The winter begins to thaw, the Earth starts to warm, the world turns its focus to spring. She is frozen in time; it is still January behind her eyes.

January 18 2015

I think I died last night. I think I was murdered. I watched it happen. I felt it happen. I am sure of it. But I am still breathing. And no one has noticed a thing.

January 19 2015

I'm frozen. Disconnected from my grief. You've robbed me even of that. My body is still shaking - Reverberations of a shocked heart, of all the tears I cannot cry. My eyes are left clear to watch you leave: to remember the way you discarded me when you were finished as one does with a cigarette. Extinguished under the weight of your body. You are smiling as you go, so hideously unscathed.

January 20 2015

None of it makes sense.
None of it is fair.
And all of it –
All of it feels as though it is someone else's life I feel so far away, so separated from myself.
Part of me wants to fall apart.
Crumble.
Because I think feeling something;
Anything at all
Even such obliterating pain

Would be better than this.

January 21 2015

I'm sitting in my car, writing this across from an empty mansion from another time, listening to classical music drip from the radio. All I want is to be transported into another world. One that is beautiful. But everything is so cold. It makes sense in a way. That everything be so barren and unforgiving.

There are paths leading from the old estate into the surrounding forest, and I want to take them, if only to get further away from where I am. No distance, however, seems to be far enough. All of these feelings of devastation, all the shuddering memories seem to have stained me, and I haven't yet found a way to wash them clean. I don't know how to purge all the convulsing, swirling darkness so turbulent inside me. I don't know whether to scream or sob IT WASN'T WHAT I WANTED. It seems as if I'm incapable of doing either. Just as there has risen such a wall between myself and other people, there seems to have also risen perhaps an even greater wall between myself and my own emotions, my own pain. I feel nothing. Just cold. Can he really be allowed to steal this from me as well? Is this what shock is? None of it, not the fact that my virginity is gone, not the fact that it was stolen, not the fact that my first time was rape – none of it has sunk in. None of it feels like my life. I feel so barred from it. Barred from feeling anything at all. Detached. None of it feels real.

You stole everything in a single thoughtless, careless, hopeless and empty instant. It should've been mine. Mine to give. Mine to enjoy, mine to remember, mine to feel; and all of this is impossible. I retreated so far inside myself, was so deeply traumatized, in shock, so all consumingly alone and empty as you slammed into me, that still, the memories come only in vivid, vicious, disconnected flashes. The feelings, all of them, I am numb to. They do not feel like my own.

Mine to enjoy? You tore through me dry. There is no denying what you did was for anyone but yourself. Mine to give? Your aggression, my hopeless abandonment, it all had me frozen. You never asked, never waited. I never had an option. There was never, from the first moment until when it was finally all over, a single instant in which I had a chance. And I can't stop shaking. I just wish this had never happened. I wish I could get it back. I wish I could cry or throw up or something. Anything. I wish I was leaving forever. Going somewhere entirely new. And never coming back.

January 22 2015

My eyes are wide with memories
Your ghost swirls in my irises, a nightmare doused in emerald green
All my midnights now are haunted
And I'm fending off sleep: Knowing once again from you; from my mind
There will be no escape

January 25 2015

I don't know what to say to you
How to tell you.

That

I'm not ok

That nothing is fine.

Why don't you notice?

Why does no one notice?

January 28 2015

I hate you for taking up so much space in my mind; real estate you do not deserve and could never afford. I see everything that I could not stop again and again behind my eyes. My body feels it in shadow flashes, dark phantom echoes: your frenzy, the way my body shook beneath you, the loudness of the silence.

I see everything. Again and again.

I dream about it too, which I detest even more. That you could be allowed to invade not only my body, my consciousness, but have forced your way into the realm of my dreams as well. The best ones, of all the nightmares, are the ones where I'm dead. It's not that you kill me necessarily. It's just that after lying there, naked, alone, and abused for you – I died. And it all makes such sense to me, in an innate, right way that I find pleasure in. It is the first thing that has made sense since that night, since you. Because it felt like I died. As if I should have.

The problem, the real problem with it all – other than the fact that I'm not dead, that I'm not in a heaven where symphonies and operas are played on beaches under blazing sunsets – the real problem is that there is no respite. There is no moment to recharge. Just surviving, passing through each day is a marathon. A performance. I am exhausted. The end of the day leaves me drained, depleted. Everything is overwhelming, overstimulating. I guess I'm still expecting, at any moment now, for it all to kill me, for it all to become too much, for my heart to give out. I feel so claustrophobic. I want out. Out of this place. This school. This bedroom. This bed. For now though, as apparently, my body is stubbornly refusing to drop dead, the only thing to do is survive. Impossibly, unreasonably, irrationally. I must find a way. And yet I do not want to. I want to crumble, surrender, cry, scream, run, implode, something, anything, just for anyone to realize, anyone to notice.

January 30 2015

There is not a single part of my soul that feels as if it wasn't stolen. Not a single part that feels like it is still my own. And that, I think, is the worst part. That suddenly, one could be flooded with grief and fury and depression and anger, and not have wanted any of it. And that it could continue, and continue and continue, long after the original crime ends.

February 1 2015

The house is empty, again, like it was then. I can't even pretend I don't hate it. I want to throw something across the room, let it hit the wall, let it shatter. I want to hit something, feel the pain in my hand, feel something, anything. Put a crack in this wretched disconnectedness or just in the silence of this empty house.

February 5 2015

I'm exhausted. I want to curl into the smallest ball possible, evaporate, become the mist that floats off the waves. I don't care about anything. And the fact that anyone has the audacity or the ignorance to think that I have energy to expend is stunning. I'm in such a state of disarray already I don't want to even try to think about anyone or anything else. I won't apologize for needing time to heal from a wound I never wanted. Is it not enough that I have to sleep every night in the bed that I was raped in? That I am surrounded constantly by people who don't know, that I must constantly act as if I am fine when I'm the furthest thing from it? Nothing is fine. Nothing. Nothing. Nothing. I hate it. I hate it here. I hate pretending. I hate being so tired, being so afraid, being so sad, being so angry. I hate it. I hate that no one notices. I need to get out of here. Somewhere far away.

February 7 2015

I am so empty. And so, I read Tolstoy's Anna Karenina and Arabian Nights, write in leather-bound journals, leaf through classic poetry, crave the sounds of a symphony, of an opera. All things entirely of a different world, a beautiful world, one in which I didn't get raped. One where my virginity wasn't stolen from me, one where I am not terrified of nights alone in my own bed. One in which I am transported. And all is well. I'm on a sleigh on the snow-covered streets of Saint Petersburg, covered in furs; I'm beneath a glowing moon shining over waves of Sahara sands, I'm reading stanzas of words that sound like music. And hoping that somehow, all of these things will salve over the gaping hole so brutally carved into my heart.

February 9 2015

I feel like I'm gonna throw up
And there's nothing poetic about it

February 19 2015

I turn off the lights and immediately I am back in that moment
Transported
Nauseous
Afraid
Numb
Helpmehelpmehelpme
Someone
Anyone
Alone
No one comes
No escape
Tear through me
Dry shaking broken
Againagainagainagain
And I'm gone
Far from anywhere
Your smile, cold

Your eyes, colder

February 22 2015

She loved abandoned things. Ruins. Crumbled walls and climbing ivy. There was a decadence in destruction. A beautiful tragedy that told a story. It was a familiar tale. It read just like her own.

February 23 2015

I am wishing for anything to concentrate on but you. Anything but what it felt like to be so horribly invaded. Penetrated. Violated. Oh god – the feeling of him inside me, Inside! It all makes me sick. Revolted. Sends me recoiling at my own memories. Wishing there was any way to purge myself of this barbary. This is all I have left. Wishes. Dreams. Nothing is real. Nothing.
Do you know you ejected me so far out of myself that I could no longer see my own reflection? I stared at the mirror, blinked slowly, comprehensively. Understanding even in that numb daze that I was gone. That wherever I was, I was not in my body. That whatever had happened, it had happened without me. Because I was not there. I looked for the face above the naked thing you had taken. And it was simply gone. A blank glass mirroring nothing at all stared back at me. They say the eyes are the windows to the soul. And I can't tell you how fitting it is that when I looked at my reflection, I had no face, no eyes at all. My soul had fled. And any windows to the inside had long since been drawn closed.

Have you ever known such disconnect, that you only become aware of the shock and trauma your body has experienced, when you realize with a modicum of mild, slow-occurring surprise, that your limbs are convulsively shaking?

Have you ever been so utterly disconnected from reality that you are slow to comprehend events even as they are happening? As if you are submerged, deep below water, watching the world pass by in a haze above the surface, miles away.

It was as if the neurons firing from muscles to brain and back again were moving in slow motion, such was the distinction in time that separated my body physically shaking, and the moment much later (seconds that were stretched out into eternities, lifetimes, an infinite expanse of rotting space), when I finally realized that the tremors that my eyes were watching wrack my lower body, my arms, this was my body convulsively shaking. This was me, terrified. This was me, utterly and completely alone and abandoned, having done my very best to handle it, this was me not being able to withstand a moment more. This was me, bleeding out. Falling apart. Dying. Crumbling and shattering and totally and entirely numb. And that, maybe, is why all I could finally manage to say was "I'm cold."

February 24 2015

Will the full realization ever hit me? Will there ever be a moment of clarity? As much as it is constantly on my mind, it still does not sink in. My virginity, gone. My choice, stolen. My body, abused. My soul, murdered. And all I have, the only thing left that cannot be taken from me, is the only thing that is ever truly of any solace. Writing.

March 11 2015

Never has there been such flight of feeling. Every last fluttering of my heart has ceased, been rendered immobile. Rage at injustice has cooled into a simple, harsh absence. A nothingness. One lacking any sort of emotion at all. I wonder how many halves of once whole hearts walk this Earth wishing that they had all their secrets back to hold, to clutch close against their chests. I wonder how many wish they could unwhisper, unhope, undream, unlove. And so, still, I say nothing.

March 15 2015

No one heard a thing.
All the while my throat was tearing from screaming,
And the taste of blood in my mouth had me so bitter
And you were wondering always why I was so angry.
But I had long since lost my voice, no longer had the words to whisper
that I wasn't angry, I was heartbroken.
Because you had watched every minute of my tragedy, hadn't blinked or turned away for even an instant,
And still, you never saw a thing.

April 5 2015

Racing

Panic

Out of control

Helpless

Afraid

Afraid

Afraid

Help me

Help me help me

Out of breath

Loud in the silence

Inhale exhale inhale exhale

No one comes

It's over

I'm cold

April 9 2015

I can't distinguish between my nightmares and my memories.

April 10 2015

All she wanted,
All she really wanted
Was to forget that night had ever happened.
But forgetting was impossible,

Even with amnesia,
She would never lose the memory
Of his hands
Upon her skin.

April 12 2015

It seemed she was always on the verge of tears these days
There were hurricanes in her eyes
And she couldn't tell if she craved a savior
Or someone to dance with in the destruction
So, she contented herself with floating across the sea at night
Letting the tides take her
Tilting her head upwards
She painted constellations all across heaven
Then closed her eyes without any fears
Knowing every wave was built upon her tears

April 24 2015

It was spring now, nearly summer even.
But you had broken her heart in January. And she still felt Cold.

April 27 2015

Knowing you has taught me a lot. Not about you. No. Your heart is still very much a mystery. It's taught me a lot about strange things, things you wouldn't think would have anything to do with that night, with what you did. Things like venomous scorpions for instance. Creatures that paralyze their victims with their poison, and simply wait patiently beside them, knowing that there is no possibility of resistance, of surviving that first initial deadly touch. Simply wait for their victim's heart to finally give out so they can devour them. I never really understood that before. Not until you.

April 28 2015

Thoughts for one day, in love...

I wish he knew. The way it hurts and offends me that he, someone I like, wants to do this to me too. How could you? I thought you liked me? That you cared? I wish he knew the way I am terrified to become someone faceless beneath him. The way I am terrified that he too will hurt me, send me flying out of control; so unsafe, so scared. That he too will send my head slamming backwards with his every movement. The way just the thought, even the word 'thrust', the very idea, concept of that motion makes me nauseous. The way the idea of someone doing that to me again makes me want to cry, to beg. Please, no. Not that. Please not that. The way it feels like being tortured. To me, it is something done to me by someone intent on using me for his own pleasure. Using me. Me, a hole for insertion.
I wish he knew that it feels like dying. It feels like I'm under attack. It feels hopeless and helpless.
It feels like drowning.

It feels violent and aggressive and cruel. It feels like I am going to explode from the inside out, like he's going to tear me open, like he might not even notice if I died beneath him, because he's pounding into me so hard.

It feels like a jackhammer. Mechanical. Harsh. Cruel. Selfish. Relentless. It feels like I can't breathe, as if I'm being crushed. As if there is no escape. As if there is a very real possibility that he could kill me. And a very definite possibility that he would not care at all. I wish he knew.

April 30 2015

What are you so afraid of? He kept asking.
And she didn't even know where to begin.

May 3 2015

I see you in empty spaces
See your smile, cold Your eyes, Colder.

May 10 2015

She felt unattached to the world. Without a tether. Like she could slip off the edge and no one would notice. Splash into the blackness of the galaxy without making a sound. Instantaneous. Like she could ripple out into space and evaporate into star dust and all the forgotten streaks airplanes leave behind. Gone.

May 16 2015

I am leaving. Graduating. It feels triumphant, victorious. Not because of finishing school, but because I'm finally getting out. Escaping. I don't have to pretend to celebrate with them. I'm skipping the ceremony. I don't want to have to pretend that I will miss this place. That I don't hate it here. That it hasn't been hell. I'm slipping away without a sound, leaving this school, this bedroom behind. Flying across the ocean, gone to a different sky.

May 17 2015
Greek Islands.

She goes somewhere where she can feel the sun on her skin. It has been 6 months since she froze under him. But she still hasn't managed to thaw. She wraps herself in golden Mediterranean light and waits to feel warm, waits to feel anything. But she is still so cold.

May 20 2015 ; Crete, Greece.

She is small, delicate, fragile, terrified of being shattered all over again. She tries so hard to be courageous. But she is a raw, wild thing, sensitive to the slightest touch, to a lingering glance. I grieve for her. For what was done to her. For that night. She is so innocent, so helpless, so scared. I am protective of her. The little girl that was torn and bruised and split open and silenced and made invisible, even in her own reflection. I hold her hand in mine, pull her to her feet, carry her in my arms until she can walk once more on her own. I promise her I will take her somewhere warm, somewhere beautiful. Somewhere where she can immerse herself in sea and sunshine. Somewhere where she can heal. And one day, her little hand will not be quite so numb, quite so cold in my own. And she will squeeze my hand back and we will look at each other, and we will say, with utmost certainty: "We're okay now."

June 22 2015 New York

They tell me I am beautiful as if this is supposed to mean something. As if it is an accomplishment, something to be proud of. They tell me I am lucky. For how could I be unhappy? Back from the Mediterranean and bound for a new home, a new job in the Pacific Islands, I am beautiful, beautiful, beautiful, and my life is golden. When in reality, I have never known love, never known intimacy, my body was stolen and robbed from me, I am always alone. They talk about it right in front of me. Sex. As if I have any idea, as if my first time wasn't murder, wasn't torture. But I should be happy. Grateful. I am lucky. I am beautiful.

I am angry and sad and all the sadder and angrier at the expectation that I should not be.

I am not the girl you think I am.

July 27th 2015
The Middle of the Pacific Ocean.

Palm trees sway above her, sand stretches out for miles, the ocean is just down the road from her house. Everyone tells her the island she lives on is paradise. That her life is perfect.

She learns that moving 5,000 miles still isn't far enough. Because she can still feel his breath on her skin.

The island becomes another reminder of everything she is trying to forget. Everything she tried to leave behind. It is small. Everyone knows everyone. They are curious about her. They want to know everything. Who she is, who she was, where she goes, why she came there. The Girl From the Mainland.

She drives to the other side of the island just to breathe. Take a walk. Go grocery shopping. Any time she wants to do anything in an effort to avoid being accosted by the questions, the eyes that seem to follow her wherever she goes. She feels trapped.

A colleague at works asks her to join him for happy hour drinks. Week after week, she offers polite excuses. She spends every night alone. One day at work he pulls her aside. She is painfully aware of the fact that they are alone in a dark room, the way her heart is slamming against her ribcage. He tells her, in detail, what he believes men are thinking when they look at her. What they want to do to her. He says he would know.

He says, he, any man would be thinking the same thing. He tells her to keep the conversation between them. "It can be our secret." He is old enough to be her father. Later that night, in the shower, the water runs cold. It has been three hours. She is still sitting on the shower floor. Wishing every part of her would disappear down the drain.

Somewhere in between hyperventilating sobs, beneath the freezing water, she comes up with another plan. A plan that will take her far away, somewhere else, across a different ocean. When her contract is up, when the year is over, she will be gone. This knowledge allows her to survive there. On the hell island. That's what she calls it. A place known for being one of the most idyllic paradises in the world. One year. And then she will be gone. She will have gotten out. Disappeared. Escaped.

August 1 2015 ; Kauai, Hawaii

I live in the most isolated place in the world. An island a thousand hurricanes away from you. I planned it like that.
So if I were destroyed
It would be by the touch of the sea.
Never by yours.
Not ever again.

August 5 2015

I met a man who whispered in my ear

"Such a beautiful girl shouldn't carry such sadness in her eyes" And I've been sitting here for hours thinking of just the right words to say

How dare you.

August 20 2015

I don't know how long I was there for

Knees pulled up to my chest

Sitting

Arms wrapped around myself

On the shower floor

Like if I stayed there long enough

God if only I didn't move

Then maybe I would become like the water vapor falling all around me

& evaporate

Disappear

Washed clean

I stayed there for hours

The water ran cold

I watched it swirl down the drain

Wondered why the feeling of your hands remains

The memory of you

My darkest stain.

August 23 2015

You ask why you haven't seen me here before. You say you would remember me. I think, you will never see me here again.

You say my eyes are beautiful and I wonder if you see the way they flit back and forth to the exit.

I force myself to breathe.

You ask me my name. I remind myself that it isn't Terrified.

Your hand rests on my thigh. I wonder where my voice has fled. Why I can't disappear along with it.

You ask me what I want to drink. Your hand moves higher. I think of answering, but doubt poison comes in a champagne glass. You decide this means tequila. It doesn't. You tell me to relax. I remember why I can't.

It is January and cold and I can see my breath as I scream, hear the silence as no one comes.

I am shivering and you put your jacket around me and grin and say I look good in your clothes.

Your jacket is heavy. It smells like cigarettes and scars and dead-of-winter screams.

I say I have to go to the bathroom. Your hand slips from my leg as I get up, its imprint burns my skin.

You watch me, impatient. You tell me to hurry. I promise that I will.

I do. I run, run like its January and I am gone.

August 31 2015

All she wanted to do was tell you how she was breaking. The way she could feel her edges crumbling, exponentially faster and faster as the sun

went down. As night got closer. The way the darkness terrified her. All she wanted was your voice. Telling her she was safe now. That you wouldn't let anything happen to her.
But she sat in the dark, biting her lips bloody to keep silent.
 She said nothing. And you never asked if she was alright. You never noticed that she wasn't.

September 6 2015

I've been working on forgiving you. Sometimes I wonder about who you were, before.
Before me.
Before we collided and you slammed into me and sent me careening off course and crashing into comets and wondering why the sky was so empty of shooting stars. Empty of anything at all.
I wonder about what made you that way. Who made you that way.
Because there has to have been a reason.
That's the hardest part, I think. Thinking that all of this was meaningless. Random. So I think there has to have been a reason.
I have to believe that.
And so, whatever made you so cold, whoever forgot to show you how to trace stars across heaven, whoever taught you that bodies are bullets primed to destroy, that hands are meant to hurt,
Not to hold,
I'm sorry.

September 23 2015

She loved to wrap herself in the ocean's arms:
It was the only touch on her skin that did not make her think of yours.

September 25 2015

What no one ever tells you is 8 months later you'll still be lying in bed at night, so nauseous with memories that you'll wonder if it's possible to throw up your heart. Because it wasn't supposed to be this way. This wasn't supposed to happen. Not to you.
No one tells you that you'll live through the hottest summer on record and still feel cold, despite blazing heat and new voices calling you beautiful. No one tells you it won't matter. That you'll cringe at compliments, that you'll hate the body they envy. Because part of you still can't stop thinking that all it ever did was bring you straight to hell. Straight to him. And you'll be furious with yourself, so angry because no matter how badly it haunts you, the realization of what happened never truly sinks in. No one tells you that you'll feel it in pieces, flashes, all over again, new, every time.
No one ever tells you that you can be 5,000 miles away and it still won't be far enough, because you can still feel his breath, hot, heavy on your skin.
No one tells you that you'll fall in love, and you'll want things that you're terrified of. And you'll be so confused because the man you love wants to do all the same things that sent you spiraling that you swore were tearing

you apart, sending every piece of your universe crumbling. And there's a part of you that just can't separate it, even though, god, you try.
No one tells you you'll sit on the shower floor for hours praying to god you'll swirl down the drain because water can't be broken. And you're so damn sick of being in pieces.

September 29 2015

Things I say to myself at 3am:

Hush don't be afraid. Go to sleep don't be afraid you're safe now it's going to be alright go to sleep. You're safe now. It will all be okay. Hush hush hush. Sleep. It will be okay. Close your eyes. Close your eyes. You're safe. It's okay. Hush. Sleep. You're safe. Safe now. Shhhh. It's okay. Sleep. I will not let anything happen to you. I will protect you. I will love you always. Sleep. Sleep. Breathe. It will all be okay. Sleep. You are safe.

October 13 2015

I hate the phrase "You stole my heart." Robbery isn't romance. You have no idea what it is to have something irreplaceable taken from you. Something you never wanted to give. You're twirling upside down and imagine it being exciting maybe. Reckless, but the exhilarating sort, an adventure. You think of tall, dark & handsome, that he'll sweep you off your feet. You have no idea of the feelings of emptiness & loss. Of violation. The way it stays with you; when another human makes you so afraid that you can't stop shaking no matter how hard you try to still your aching limbs. You know nothing of the way you will not be able to see your own reflection in the mirror, having wished so desperately to disappear that you've gone half mad. The way you'll stare right at the glass. And see nothing at all. And you'll still feel cold. For months afterwards.

You don't think about that. They never do. That it'll block out the sun. Robbery isn't romance. And tall and handsome won't matter when all you're left with is the darkness.

October 24 2015

She still thought about it. All the time. She did not remember it like it was yesterday. She remembered it like time did not exist, as if it never had.

October 27 2015

You will cry until your head feels like it's going to explode from behind your eyes and your throat will close with untaken sobs until you choke as if you're under water and it will be the only thing that makes sense because you will feel like you're drowning because the memories will come in waves, but like the ocean, they will fill all the spaces in between as well.

It will still cause you physical pain to think about the fact that no one came.

Even now, it shocks you slightly, every time you think of it. No one came.

To think about the fact that it happened in spite of what you wanted, that it didn't matter what you wanted, that you didn't matter at all. That you could be so completely irrelevant in something so completely intimate. You.Did.Not.Matter.
To think of how alone you were then. How completely and utterly abandoned and how right now, alone on this god forsaken island, a tiny rock in the middle of the biggest ocean in the world, it doesn't feel any different.

It's okay. Remember that it is different.

How you're still terrified of mirrors, of staring at the glass and seeing nothing. Because it made you feel nonexistent. Dead. And sometimes the memories will hurt so badly you will wonder why you're not. You will wonder at how it's physically plausible for a human who was rendered so helpless and weak to have survived all of this.

It's okay. Give your courage credit. This is not the first time you have had to be brave.

And you will just want someone to hold you and stroke your hair and rub your back and say that you're safe now and they're here and they won't let anything happen to you. You will just want to believe them.

But the reality is that you will have to calm yourself down, ease your own breathing, make your own tea and hum sweet things to yourself as you rock back and forth, your own arms clutching your knees and your own voice whispering that it will all be okay one day.

Because broken pieces will simply lay broken on the floor if no one picks them up and puts them back together again, piece by piece. And no one is coming. And you will hope that all the soothing words you will sing to yourself aren't lies. Because on nights like these it will all hurt too much and it will be too heavy and too hard, and you will not want to be this forever. This scared sad shattered thing. You will not want to be this at all.

November 14 2015

Paris Terror Attacks:

It is the worst sort of crime, I think, to rob a person of their sense of safety. To cram fear down throats until innocent lives are choking with it, suffocating on a horror they never asked for. Violence, in any form, is a violation of our most basic and precious humanity, of the small moments most essential to the fabric of this experience we have named life: Drifting off to sleep unplagued by nightmares, strolling quiet streets at dusk unafraid, to go out to the theater, to fall in love with strangers on rooftops in a city named for light. It all belongs to us. We have a right to live these moments without tossing and turning, without quickening steps, without looking over our shoulder. From one victim of a robbery to another, you have my heart Paris.

January 15 2016

They tell you what doesn't kill you will make you stronger.
What they don't tell you is before you are stronger you will be the weakest you have ever been. What they don't tell you is before you are stronger you will be numb.
You will be completely and utterly haunted and shattered and you will have never thought that you could be so thoroughly and entirely broken. Before you are stronger you will be reduced to the smallest, most crumpled version of yourself. And then you will be asked to pick yourself up.
To smile while you do it.
And you will.

January 15 2016

I thought I was invincible. I was actually so deluded, so spoiled by the rose-colored world I had been born into, that I actually believed, I mean really believed- even in the face of knowledge completely contradictory- that it wouldn't happen. Not to me. It wouldn't happen. He wouldn't do that, I would escape, someone would come. Someone would come and save me. Rape did not exist in my reality.
And part of the trauma, part of the horror in the numbing aftershocks, was that this naive, childlike perspective I had, was blown apart. The world would not be kind, would not be polite, I was not immune. I was not, in fact, safe. What I wanted did not, in fact, matter. I was

insignificant. I was nothing. And people could not be trusted. I could not even be trusted with my own physical safety.

And even now, a year later, one of the most traumatizing aspects of all of it is that no one came. And that I really believed that someone would. In general, I held that belief: the insufferable hope that even in the face of certain defeat, somehow, someway, impossibly, against all odds, it wouldn't happen. Someone would come. Someone would save me. It wouldn't happen. If I didn't want it to happen, it would not. Alone, and drugged and naked, his body twice the size of mine on top of me- even then. Someone would come. Somehow, this would not take place. It could not take place. This could not be happening to me, and so it would not. It would not happen. And then he was tearing through me: my body along with every last shred of innocence I had. And part of me was ruthlessly and violently and abruptly murdered. And I was not in my body. I was watching it all happen, frozen. Helpless. Watching myself being torn open, pounded into. Fast, violent, careless. A frenzied, ruthless jackhammer. And after, my reflection was gone.

And I was not even surprised.

Can you imagine that?

Looking in a mirror and being entirely unsurprised to find your reflection utterly not there to look back at you?

Because I was not there at all. And wherever I went, even a year later, that part of me has not returned. And I do not think it ever will.

January 16 2016

We devote a lot of time to telling our children never to give up hope. Which theoretically might have been fine if I hadn't been the variety of child that was exceedingly in love with words, if they didn't seep into my bloodstream like a drug and intoxicate my soul. Fairytales flowed through my every nerve ending. I existed in a place where it was eternally summer and Januaries were a remote thing, a distant vaguery I hardly believed in. Wrapped in paper and ink armor, I thought I was invincible. I was actually so deluded, so enamored of the stories I had read, so confident in the sense of safety that had lulled me so easily to sleep for twenty one years, all the pretty things I had been told, that I actually believed, I mean really believed- even in the face of knowledge completely contradictory - that it wouldn't happen. Not to me. It wouldn't happen. It was infinitely more plausible, in the instances before my universe was destroyed, that time would stop. That a celestial being would intervene on my behalf; that the galaxy itself would bend and fold according to my will.

And then, in the space of the next second, lifetimes and millennia later, all the pretty words exploded. Every story blown apart. Because until far beyond the last, fatal moment; in a sickening, horrible, twisted way - I had believed in hope.

But no one was coming.

No one.

And fairytales, finally, were just that.

January 16 2016

I know it's just a day like any other but I can't stop watching the clock...I can remember exactly what I was doing a year ago now and how normal everything was and then exactly what time everything started happening, how long it lasted, exactly what it felt like and it's like I'm watching it happen to myself all over again. And I'm just as frozen and helpless and useless as I was then except for this time I know how it all ends.

January 17 2016

I see myself, the girl I was a year ago, moving through moments and hours and the neat boxes of calendar days that would bring her- bring me- to that night. And I want to stop her. But I cannot do anything. I watch, I am silent. I have proven to be good at that.

She wasn't even going to go out that night. It was cold. It was late. She was alone. Her best friend, the one she had come out to be with was with her boyfriend. And she was left with strangers who wanted to touch her, talk to her, buy her drinks. The conversation lasted too long she was too alone too far from everyone that she knew; he was too close, too determined. All of a sudden, she is in a cab with him, alone. She doesn't know how she got there. It didn't even seem odd to her then, that she was numb. Even though she had only had one drink. It struck her in a tilted sort of way at the bar when he told her she was not drunk enough, yet. Yet. And later the premeditation would make her nauseous. She would go into an empty house, left alone with the boy that was going to rape her. Her bra hit the floor. White. Lace. Dead. He pulled her jeans off.

Her underwear torn away. He was heavy. She was frozen. Someone was coming, weren't they? This couldn't be allowed to happen could it? No one came. He was inside her. Inside her. She was being murdered. She couldn't move. Couldn't scream. Couldn't breathe. Jackhammer. Every thrust sends her head pounding against the windowsill behind her it is a frenzy her voice is a constant quiet stream of how much it hurts it hurts it hurts it hurts you're hurting me. If he hears her, it doesn't matter. It doesn't stop. She doesn't realize she is convulsively shaking until she sees her limbs quivering uncontrollably, she cannot feel her body, she is detached. No one came.

"I'm cold". It is all she is able to say. Faceless in the mirror. She wasn't there. Standing in front of the glass naked numb and quite clearly seeing a body without a face. Reflectionless. Gone.

Dead. Silent. He kisses her.

Sleeping in the bed where he had robbed her of her soul. Dreaming that she had died. Attending her own funeral. And for the first time feeling peace.

Completely and entirely numb. Bruised. Swollen beyond recognition. Telling doctors she was fine because she couldn't take her clothes off in front of anyone, even when she was alone, she closed her eyes. Her body disgusted her. Everything hurt and yet she couldn't feel anything at all. Taking the plan B pill the next day. Everything is a blur now. White paper on doctor tables. Enduring comments from the STD test nurse who didn't know, "anything else I can do for you? Maybe just some condoms?" Writing Emailsemailsemails postponing her internship due to a "sudden and unforeseeable personal crisis." Asuddenandunforeseeablepersonalcrisis personalcrisispersonalcrisis.

The words swirl around her head like vultures. She goes home for the weekend. Curled up in her childhood bed, removed, exiled forever from her own childhood.

Her mother: Did you say no? Well, darling, how was the poor boy to know?

Even now. Every time she looks at a mirror, it is on her mind. She hesitates. She starts slow, eyes flicker up, bottom to top. Terrified that once she looks up, where her face should be, she won't be there. Again. Even now she cannot say the word rape. She says, "What Happened in January." January is synonymous with what happened. It is cold it is dark it is numb. Because even though logically she knows she would not be so traumatized still, had it been anything else, there is part of her that feels like a fraud. That constantly and continuously whispers that what happened in January was a failure on her part. She did not protect herself. Did she even try?

Darling, How was the poor boy to know?

And so on the nights when she has panic attacks when she cannot stop the hyperventilating sobs, when she lays in bed wrapped under covers in eighty degree weather, when she sits on the shower floor, rocking back and forth, arms wrapped around herself, after it ends when she sings and hums to herself and rubs her own back and makes her own tea, there is a part of her that feels relieved. Because it must be true.

January 29 2016

I wonder if you could've possibly imagined. When you were slamming into me, when you were on top of me. I wonder if you could've possibly imagined, that the thing beneath you, was a person. That a year later, that person would still lie awake at night, sobbing at the memory of your touch.

I wonder if you could've possibly imagined that you would be the star of my nightmares,

that even when my eyes were open, you would be there, my skin betraying me with echoes of memories that refuse to fade.

I wonder if you could've imagined.

I wonder if you knew.

I wonder if it would've made any difference.

January 31 2016

There is something so horribly exhausting in always being the one to save yourself. This is the feeling I believe; we are supposed to know as being "empowered".

But sometimes, you're just tired. You're so tired and it all hurts so much, and you just wish, just for a minute you didn't have to be brave and you didn't have to be strong and you could count on someone else to be there. Someone else to pull you from the wreckage, to raise you up, lift you out of the ashes. For someone else to save you. You wish you could be the girl that gets rescued. You wish you could be the girl that gets scooped up and swirled away, you wish that all your shadows could become midnight magic in His eyes, & that that would make them feel the slightest bit lighter on your shoulders.

February 6 2016

Staff meeting, at work:

It was a small thing. Just an offhanded comment. Casual. But it took her straight back there, and suddenly her feet were taking her up and out of the room because all of a sudden he was touching her again and she could feel his breath on her neck and then she was crying. No sobbing, the kind without any sound at all, doubled over in a bathroom stall without any real idea as to how she had gotten there. And she didn't know how long it lasted, just that once her body had stopped shaking, she decided that the only possibility left to her, the only remotely conceivable thing to do, was to watch the sun set over the sea. And imagine she could disappear over the horizon along with it.

February 14 2016

A day at the beach:

I don't think you meant to ruin her day.
I don't think you meant to, but you did.
And I'm telling you now because maybe you'll remember this the next time.
For the next girl that catches your eye.
That makes you nudge your friends
Laugh
About how good you imagine she is. All the things you want to do to her

While she pretends she doesn't hear.
For the next time you saunter over
Ask her if she is here by herself
She loses her page in the book she is reading.
You are too close.
She is all too conscious of the skin that is showing
She wishes she was covered in layers and layers of clothing.
The hand you place on her shoulder "You're pretty."
All of her muscles are tense and rigid and she feels just like she did then and it is 87 degrees and palm trees are waving above her but inside of her it is January and cold and she is screaming and suffocating and numb all at once.
She lets you talk to her for a few minutes, offers a smile that feels like it costs everything that makes up her soul before she says she doesn't mean to be rude, but she has to finish her book.
She feels as if she has to say that.
"I don't mean to be rude."
She doesn't look up to see if you have gone. She keeps her head down, body tense and rigid. Much the same as if she is being stalked by a wild animal. No sudden movements. Don't do anything to provoke it. Be still. Invisible. She remains frozen until she hears the laughter and whistles fade away.
It takes all of her concentration to keep from shaking.
She tries to find her place in the book, tries to remember the story, tries to feel warm, to feel safe. But her breathing is coming too fast and she can no longer feel the sun on her back and five minutes later she is driving home, even though she hasn't been to the beach in forever, even though

she's been looking forward to the sun and sand all week, even though you are gone. Because she can still feel your eyes on her skin. Because they feel like his. And because she is so sick of being stared at, and not seen at all.

February 28 2016

Do you have any idea how exhausting - how empty it is
To always be wanted, forever desired, But never Løved.

March 12 2016

You stare at me like my skin is made of gold.
Like it would shimmer under your touch
And you can't stop watching
Not for a moment
Because when the lights go out
I might glitter
Like all of the galaxies you imagine I am made up of
An alien.
From a universe away
A place where they don't feel any pain.

May 1 2016

The thing they don't ever really tell you is that it doesn't stop.

Long after everyone else's world has steadied, turned right side back up again,
Yours is still blown apart.
You are still standing amidst the rubble and just breathing seems like an accomplishment.
But next to you people are going about their fully saturated lives and you are frozen, black and white. And you'll watch them from the other side of an impossibly thick glass that they will not notice at all, and you will find it remarkable, the way color has never felt more foreign or far away. And by this time, they have assumed you are "fine" again, if they ever knew anything was amiss at all. The word fine will have lost all sense of meaning for you. If you falter for even a second they will ask with renewed concern what's wrong, as if there must be something other, as if there could be anything else, as if the thing that slammed into you and shattered your world couldn't possibly still be relevant. They have moved on. Their lives are in motion, accelerating, vibrant. And it will seem impossible to you. It did to me. But you can't blame them, not really. They don't know any better. The taste of grief after all, after its short burst of romantically tragic, mysterious glamour, becomes so exhaustingly stale.

May 9 2016

"Panic attack." The phrase is so overused. Do you even know what it means?

Immediate.

A wave of nausea,

Of dread

And fear. Fear because you feel Helpless.

Helpless.

All of a sudden it is January in the middle of May

and his hands are touching you

And your bra hits the floor

White

Lace

Dead

Cold

Silence and jackhammers and how you never thought those two things could go together until that night.

But that doesn't seem that strange, now that you think about it:

Nothing made sense that night.

And right now it feels the same and you just want to

Disappear

To go up in smoke

You honestly don't care

If your existence

Your entire being evaporated off the map

Here one second

Gone the next

Because right now

Existence feels so painful

so brutally

hopeless and destitute and lonely and forsaken and lost
That not existing seems like the only thing in the world that might hurt less

May 25 2016

The thought of you nauseates me.
I have blocked most of you out
You are a blur
I see your shadow on the edge of my vision
You are flickerings
Flashes inside my nightmares
There is a singer who looks just like you
I remember laughing about it
When you were still just a tall silhouette of a dark stranger on the other side of the bar.
I can no longer listen to his music without the urge to vomit.
I have shoved your name beyond the reaches of my consciousness. I am so grateful to have successfully repressed anything that could make you any more real, any more human. It is easier to think of you as a monster. Because there are all too many things all too real that have resisted repression.
Your weight. So much heavier than my own. I can still feel it crushing my frame. Your voice. Some nights, at 3 am or when I'm out to lunch and someone walks too close to me, I can feel your breath: hot, poisonous against my neck, my ear. Your hands. The way they destroyed and discarded my clothes, left ashes of my soul scattered in my sheets. Your

frenzied horrific violence, your jackhammer silence. The way you kissed me at the end, when you decided you were finished, what it is to be frozen and devastated and shaking and bleeding and bruised; what it is to be kissed by lips that have killed you.

You never had to block me out. You do not remember me at all. You never knew my name, there is nothing to fear or recall. But heaven help you if you ever have a kid

A little baby girl, and in her eyes,

You remember what you did.

June 2016, Somewhere Over the Pacific Ocean

She is leaving. Finally. Every subsequent instant that passes, she is soaring further and further away from the island she has lived on for the past year. She watches out of the plane window as the island fades away into nothingness behind her. She is smiling. She swears that she will never go back. For the first time in a long time, she is excited for everything that she is heading towards. She is hopeful. This time, she thinks, she has finally gotten it right. This will be more than an escape. This will be more than somewhere to run away to. This will be somewhere to stay. Somewhere to be happy. A month back in New York, just enough time to leave again, and then she will be gone to Paris, gone to another world. She swears, in this one, things will be different.

June 6 2016, New York

He always wondered how someone that looked like she had been handed everything on a silver platter, could simultaneously be so afraid of the world.

She wondered how he could fail to understand that "pretty" is the most dangerous thing that could happen to a girl.

June 9 2016

A letter I never sent:

Mr. Turner,

You said that your son has already paid "a steep price for 20 minutes of action" 20 minutes?

I do not know if these are the wishful delusions of a bereft father, or an indication of an outrageously irresponsible, egocentric, and sickening naiveté.

If only.

If only the consequences of rape lasted simply as long as the action. For me, that night, I felt as though even the action would go on forever. But it ended. It did. I do not know if it was after minutes or after hours of being rendered helpless, a shadow of myself, forced from my own body by an action so repugnant and traumatizing that I was in and out of consciousness, lucid, watching frozen and numb from above as I was torn apart, torn open, below. Minutes or hours? Time ceased to exist. But it did end.

And I suppose you were thinking, when you made that comment, how devastating, even if it had gone on all night, how devastating could minutes or hours really be in comparison to a life forever altered by a jail sentence?

How devastating?

It has been one year, four months and 22 days since I was raped on the same night as your son's victim, Mr. Turner.

I can tell you there has not been one minute or hour that has been the same for me since.

In the instants after the assault, my body and mind riddled and paralyzed by shock and trauma, I found myself, bruised, swollen and disfigured, in front of a mirror; only to find it reflection-less. For the life of me, I could not see my face in the glass. I suppose it was a result of feeling so entirely as if what had just occurred had killed me. As if I no longer existed in the world at all. I live still, in fear of looking at mirrors, terrified of what I might not find there. I have been unable to watch movies or listen to music with any mention whatsoever of a man's desire for a woman, without breaking down into tears. I have sat, legs dangling off the white paper of hospital tables, waiting to find out what physical damage lay beneath the filth on my skin. I have been kept up at night with nightmares, haunted during the day by flash-backs. I have been numb, disconnected, hollow. At 21 years old, I have felt alien on a college campus where partying is painted rose-colored, and where the environment perceived by so many to be fun, is the setting of my nightmares. My body has convulsively shaken. I have vomited at memories. I have been unable to be alone with a man without feeling unsafe. I have sat on my shower floor and sobbed, praying to god that I might evaporate into the steam, swirl down the drain, to, over a year later, finally feel clean. I have moved 5,000 miles away from everyone and everything that I knew, so desperately did I require an escape. I moved 5,000 miles to learn that there is no escaping your own body, nor the demons that haunt it.

Mr. Turner, your son is that demon to another girl like me.

I have had panic attacks, been unable to breathe for racking, hyperventilating sobs, noises so inhuman, I have wondered how they manage to come from my body at all. I cringe at gentle touches from friends or family. I have curled up, numb, on my childhood bed, exiled forever from the innocence of childhood. I will never have the luxury of knowing physical intimacy untainted by the memories of rape, the only experience in a virgin's repertoire. I have been unable to imagine sex existing in a way that is not horribly violent. I will never be able to have an intimate relationship with someone who does not know and understand this darkest stain on my past.

The world I knew and lived in before is gone, eradicated forever from existence. Those "moments or hours" have irrevocably changed the fabric of my entire universe. The shadow of that night stretches long and dark, and even after therapy and the support of friends and family, I know that it will be there for the rest of my life.

"His life has been deeply altered"?

I hope so. Maybe this is an indication that, somewhere within the person that shattered a woman's sense of dignity, worth, safety, security, self, femininity, and humanity, there exists a soul with conscience and a chance for redemption.

"His every waking minute is consumed with worry, anxiety, fear and depression"?

If your son truly feels the extent of guilt that he should, a guilt that accounts for the true length and duration of the consequences of sexual assault, an amount that extends far beyond twenty minutes, but that exists for a lifetime, I can almost feel sympathy for him. Because understanding the gravity of his crime, the reality of what he has done to another human; a person entirely innocent and undeserving and unsuspecting of the dark one-way turn he forced her world to take, is a much harder thing, I think, to live with, than even the longest jail sentence.

So you can imagine my confusion, my utter derision, indignation and fury at the idea that a six month sentence might be too much to bear. Because if he truly comprehended what he had done, or if you had the slightest understanding of the magnitude and implications of the crime your son has perpetrated, you would know the sentence is laughably microscopic in comparison to the one that should always weigh upon his conscience, as well as entirely insignificant in comparison to the sentence that he forced upon his victim from the moment he touched her.

Sincerely.

July 13 2016

And all of a sudden everything was dark and swirling and I was cold and the people around me, the people who have no idea that the temperature of my universe has just plummeted into an ice age of memories, of haunted nightmares, they are still laughing. Oblivious. And so I smile too, even though it feels frosted, as though it might drive a crack deep into me, even though I wonder if I will shatter. Because this, jokes about sex, it will never be funny to me. It will never not be a reminder of being raped. It will never not be a reminder of being bruised beyond recognition, disfigured. Made to be in pain, hardly able to walk for days after. Being hurt by someone else. Limping around that campus, the place whose very nature had allowed it to happen. White paper on doctor's tables. Terrified of the naked body I felt so detached from. Reflectionless mirrors.

Numb. Darkness. Feeling nauseous, terrified to ride a bike after it made me sore in the same place, echo memories, immediate, fast, dizzying, silent. They have no idea. The way they talk about the same thing, the very same thing that nearly killed me, sex, the same thing that still haunts every shadowed moment and space, that seeps into every crack - the way they talk about this same thing with laughter and light hearts and commiserating glances, as if I know these things too, as if I should also find them funny, find them just as amusing. But I share no common ground. I have never had these experiences. I am of a different universe entirely, an alien girl. I look just like them, and they believe that I am. But I am not and can never be. I am scarred from their planet, the place where these conversations and glances are painted lush and thrilling. From their rose flooded world, I share only the thorns. And it is their stabbing pain that surfaces when our two universes collide. They see nothing. I feel everything. And all of a sudden, I cannot breathe. All of a sudden, I am cold. It is dark. January. I am alone. Battered. A remnant disposed. And I cannot breathe. Dizzy. I am reminded of the worst moments. Sobbing at sex scenes during romantic comedies. Unable to listen to songs with even the briefest mention of a man's desire. How far I have come and how much some things still hurt, how it brings me right back there, how I fear that it always will. That night cast such a long shadow. And I wonder how far into the future it will stretch, or if it will go on forever. Eternity. Will there ever be a time where this feels distant? Where it is not overwhelmingly tragic and horrifying and violent and terrifying?

July 15 2016

You saw me shatter.
I have to remind myself of this.
That you were there.
That you were in my bedroom when I turned up that day at the end of January unexpected, unannounced and out of nowhere.
That you were there when I fell to pieces in front of you, when I crumbled. True, the incident was isolated.
I picked myself back up quickly, you swept the broken pieces under the rug. One weekend and I was gone again. I recovered out of sight and earshot and no one has spoken of that moment since. It is almost as if it never happened at all. Almost.
I suppose I cannot blame you for your ignorance.
You never saw me terrified to go to sleep at night, you never knew I rearranged all my furniture at 3am, just to feel slightly less haunted. You were not there for the doctor appointments, the blood that was drawn, the paper-topped tables, the clinical voices. You never saw me treated as a statistic. You never heard my screams wake me from my own nightmares. You never saw me hyperventilate. You never saw me numb, or the way I withdrew from everyone, everything. You never knew of the nausea, the flesh memories, the flashbacks. You never knew of the music I could no longer listen to, the movies I could no longer watch, the places I no

longer wanted to go, the parties I no longer attended, jokes I no longer found funny. The long drives I took, contemplating in a reflective sort of manner, how easy it would be to simply drift into the other lane of traffic. You never knew of the dreams I had about being dead. How they were the only ones I awoke from calm. You never knew about the panic attacks in the bathroom stall at work. You never listened to me cry myself to sleep for nights on end. You never saw me turn into an insomniac, memorize my ceiling. 47 tiles. The stain in the left corner from too harsh a winter. You never knew I sat on the shower floor for hours, until the water ran cold, praying to be washed clean.
You never asked, and I never told.
So I have to remind myself, that you were there, or wonder if your heart is simply just that cold.

June 21 2016

She laughed at people who said they could drown their demons. She had always found this solution to be exceedingly foolish. As if anything that could exist inside her, anything tenacious enough to both survive and devastate her tempest soul, wouldn't, at the very least, know how to swim.

July 28 2016

You asked me if I had gotten over it yet. Over brunch.
Polite, in between sips of tea.
And that's when I knew that you had never understood the reality, the fundamental essence of what had happened.

Because if you had understood even partially, if you had comprehended even the slightest bit, than you would never have asked at all, you would've known that your question made as little sense as midnight does, the middle of the night being the first moment of morning. You would've known that one does not simply "get over" something like that. One does not simply forget. It seems as though remembering how to forget is the only thing I cannot recall. Because there is a midnight ingrained on my mind and stained upon my soul and it made no more sense come the next morning or any that have followed.

How does one get over freezing? Eventually, of course, you thaw. But how could you think that I would not always hold the memory of that cold? They amputate limbs for frostbite, did you know that? Such a pity isn't it, that they cannot amputate a heart. Because even standing once again in the sunlight, I could never forget what it is to be numb, to have ice seep into my bloodstream, saturate my veins until you could've skated across the cracks between atrium and ventricle. I think you would've enjoyed that. It is so easy to imagine you twirling on a blade across my heart. How could it be that you thought I could be rendered half-dead; and wake up the next morning unaffected by the knowledge that being rescued is a myth, a fairytale. A fantasy of children. Useless. How could it be that you thought I would get over being left so entirely alone. That I could forget shaking uncontrollably, unable to recognize my own limbs, unable to see my own reflection. That I could forget thinking I was dead. How could I live once ice had been inside me? Mine was a summer-soul, surely this January violation spelled murder, surely this was something you understood - But you didn't. You don't.

Another sip of your tea, a tactful change of topic. You call for the waiter, something upon which to fall, order off the menu for me; try to convince yourself you know me at all.

July 11 2016

Had it never occurred to them that there had been moments so devastatingly empty, so horrifically numb, that she would always be drawn to what was beautiful, radiant, vibrant? Fine art, the opera, symphonies. Just as if these things were a lifeline, as if her heart had remained in January, just as if she was still in desperate need of saving? I suppose it is so much simpler to believe that she is stuck up.

August 7 2016

It's rather sick, isn't it?
I suppose I was jealous that all of her pain and chaos and madness came from somewhere so close to the surface that she could manage to speak of it.
Whereas I have never been able to drudge my own from where it exists at the deepest, most hellish corners of my soul.

August 22nd 2016 Paris, France

She immerses herself in another language, another culture, another world. She is someone else here. She is separate, apart, away. She disconnects herself from everyone and everything from that place. The nothing town. Her home. She cannot bear to be that person any longer. Numb. Shattered. Destroyed.

She surrounds herself with beauty, wears it like armor against that night: art museums, operas, delicate iron-wrought balconies, ballets, ornate palaces, sunsets over rooftops. Someone shows her that it is possible to be touched without crumbling. He is patient every time she freezes. Gentle. Kind. And eventually she starts to thaw. She is healing. She is happy again. She likes who she is here. She never wants to leave. She never wants to go back.

September 30 2016

It was in her eyes
A flicker, a shadow
Something there, and then gone
She'd never told him of the things
She'd seen
And he'd never needed to ask.

He was good at reading people, he'd said.
And she was a girl with a past.

October 7 2016

She said take me somewhere, he told her hold on tight
And her hands went around his waist and she pressed
Herself against his back and
They sped around the rings of Saturn;
The wind whipping through her hair

October 11 2016

He told her he didn't know if he was ever going to find her. She asked where he had been looking and he swore that he had walked the entire Earth. She laughed and told him that was the problem – she was in the sea, could only be found within its waves, in the silver moonlight falling across the shore, in comets shooting across the sky over midnight depths, in ancient currents, golden tides, all the lost constellations between hemispheres. She told him to search for her in the waters below Jupiter and Saturn, that the place where the ocean shifts from blue to
green is where she would be found – he said he didn't know how to swim,
And
she told him the best way to learn is to drown.

October 15 2016

Forgive them, darling, but don't forget.
Chase sunsets and laugh
From away across the sea,

Let the scars they gave you glow
In the moonlight as you lay back,
Cradled among the stars
Because they will never know this feeling
And because you knew it all along.

October 20 2016

There was a time when I thought I couldn't take the physical pain that comes with the thought of you for a moment longer. I have never been so happy to be sleeping an ocean away. My lips speak a different language, one that you would not understand, and the universe in which you collided into me has never felt so distant. The sun is shining on the rooftops outside my window and there are old men in the park drinking wine in the shade and there is a river running through a tower of iron lace and there is a kitten climbing a trellis of roses in the garden and I am weightless and I feel free.

October 24 2016

You murdered a bit of her soul that night, do you know that?
And I wonder, how does it feel, to know your hands are stained with the blood of a broken heart.

November 4 2016

"Aren't we all though?" She asked.

"All what?" He said, wondering where her voice went when it trailed off, what her eyes were seeing when the turquoise pools glazed over and froze.

"Haunted." She finished simply.

November 5 2016

It was the first time you saw her. It was before you knew her name or had heard her laugh, before you knew her favorite place to hide, before you ever saw her cry, before you became addicted to her sighs, before you stayed up all night reading her favorite book, just to try to understand her mind.

It was back before any of this. And she had been beautiful, so much so that it was distracting. But you couldn't help but notice that there was something heavy in the way she stood. And maybe it was the champagne, but more than anything, the first thing you had thought, that very first time you saw her, was that she looked like a desert flower.

Gone too many years without rain.

November 6 2016

She is skittish, a wild animal. She is acutely aware of his every breath, the way his eyes follow her curves. She is a feral creature, and her body will not allow her to forget the way his species is inherently dangerous to her own.

November 7 2016

If eyes are windows into the soul, I hope you see hurricanes every time you look at me.

November 8 2016

The problem isn't being called beautiful. It's never being called anything else.

Tell me a soul like mine is like finding an oasis in the desert, tell me I am intelligent, that what you would do to hear my laugh one more time would put the most dependent addict to shame. Tell me I am kind, tell me that oceans are not half so deep nor complex nor mysterious nor volatile, tell me I am brave, tell me that you admire the way my heart beats for bodies outside of my own, tell me that you pray every night for constellations that are half as bright as my eyes when I'm looking at you, tell me I am no more meant to be perfect than this galaxy that blew itself up to create time and planets and stars and you and I.

November 11 2016

She was without a doubt a product of the chaos of the world, and was all the more intriguing to those who watched her for the way shadows fell haphazardly across her face, and the truth slipped sporadically from her mouth, and the way she wondered about infinity and what part in it she played. She was a dark satin stroke of lightning and the smell of charcoal and embers never left her skin. They should've taken notice then, should've wondered, should've asked themselves, asked her – where her darkness, that smell of charcoal came from, they should have asked her if she had been burned.

November 13 2016

How many more times would it have to happen – her body seized by panic, her mind drenched in memories, heart paralyzed – before she remembered that she was not a normal girl. She could not do normal things. Normal was hell to her. She was allergic to this place; Earth, men. And all that they did for pleasure made her feel like dying and she could no longer remember how to breathe, even though, with you, she wants to.

November 17 2016

Everything you are is dangerous to me. And yet, still, I tiptoe closer, just as if everything you are did not shatter me. Just as if I am not terrified. Because maybe, impossibly, you are different.

November 30 2016

Her heart was a dark melody – something raw and soft and strange and foreign played on octaves set too far apart.
And so, she spent her days wandering the world, searching for someone whose hands could hold her; someone whose fingertips could span the keys.

December 6 2016

Every time they call her beautiful rather than her name, she feels her heart turn a little more to stone.

December 8 2016

She could never describe entire days. Her mood flickered in time with moments, which themselves were not associated with time. Not in any conventional way. She was not a conventional girl.
She could only tell you that there had been a particular shaft of afternoon light that had entered her room through the white lace of her curtains, and it had caused her to look up, to gaze out across the rooftops at the vastness of the sky, just beginning to be tinged with sunset gold. She could tell you that it made her wonder how many other people were staring up at the sky at that same moment, remarking upon its beauty, and if the sky did not ever grow weary of being appreciated only for the way she looked when she was glowing and resplendent and dressed up at night.
If perhaps that was why the sky swirled into hurricanes and tornadoes and threw lightning strikes and sobbed monsoons upon an Earth that only ever stared and called her beautiful; when in fact, she was layer upon layer of atmosphere,
And needed only for one person to notice.

December 12 2016

I guess I hope one day, you realize.
What you did.
I hope it hits you all of a sudden
When you are in the produce aisle of a grocery store
And you lose your breath and you drop what you are holding
And suddenly you are left
Picking green bell peppers off the floor and pretending
It's not a memory that's making your eyes sting.
I hope one day you realize.

December 15 2016

One day it will be late morning on a Saturday in summertime and he will be half asleep still and the sky will be amber and pink outside the curtains you forgot to close the night before. He will stretch and pull you closer and you will be laying against his chest and listening to his heart beating and you will not be afraid. You will finally feel safe.

December 18 2016

Some nights, she was not poetic at all.
There was nothing velvet in her darkness, no satin to her shadows, there was nothing beautiful or romantic, no metaphor in her tragedy - it was just void of light. It was just ugly. It just hurt.
There is nothing pretty

About being nauseous at your own memories, wanting to claw your way out of your own skin, cringing at your own reflection in the mirror- hoping that there will be one, remembering when there wasn't- that horrible, silent sound the human mouth produces when it is caught between a sob and a scream.
There is nothing pretty.
There is nothing at all.

December 18 2016

It is so maddening, so agonizingly frustrating, this absurd dance between fear and desire; pushing you away when I want nothing more than to pull you close. And yet still, you stay. You stay.

December 23 2016

I thought I knew. I held the kind of assuredness that you have in things that you believe in with utmost certainty, because you have never known anything else. Because it is just the way that they are. The way you believe in things like gravity and tomorrow and your next breath. I was confident. I thought I knew what it meant, I thought I knew what it felt like.

But you were so gentle, and I didn't disappear, and this, it was entirely different and not at all the same thing and I didn't know it could be this way. I didn't know this existed. And suddenly I became acutely aware that what had happened before was another thing entirely. Of another dimension, another world, another universe. If there had ever been any doubt about what he had done, it was gone. It had been a thing of darkness, of violence, of selfishness, and it had nothing at all to do with this; with you, with me, with love.

December 29 2016

"Weren't you terrified?" He said. He gazed at her, confused at the fragile creature in front of him that feared things like the dark and the touch of a man's hands on her skin, but who wasn't the least bit afraid to fly around the world on her own. "No." She said, gazing back at him serenely. "I was alive."

January 2 2017

It is the coldest, darkest month of the year and the world and my heart are frozen, numb.
"You'll never find me here!"
I wake up screaming from my nightmare.
Hazy haunting flashes
Did you have any idea how many times I would drown in them?
I am awake now. Sometimes it takes a moment to realize.
Awake. Here. Now. Safe.
Not paralyzed. Not frozen.
I stretch anyway, to be sure.
"You'll never find me here" I whisper to myself again.
And you won't.

You have no idea who I am.

I was nothing to you then, I am less than that now. I am across an ocean and a hemisphere

And in someone else's arms and safe.

I repeat this to myself over and over and over and over and over and over and over.

Safe. Safe. Safe.

Until the words sound like my own breath.

Until I almost believe it.

January 3 2017

Marble skin and a heart of stone
God she's a beautiful girl

But she's always alone.

January 4 2017

We're both laughing and I say maybe you're just easy to please. & Inside I'm begging you to tell me it's got nothing to do with that. That I'm not such a difficult and dark and broken thing. That I'm not so impossible a creature to love. That anyone would be lucky to scratch themselves on the shattered pieces of my heart if it means they get to hold me close.

But you just sling an arm around me, nonchalant, grin, say yeah, you're lucky I'm easy. And I laugh again so I don't fall apart.

January 9 2017

Hang on tight to your courage darling, these are the darkest nights of the year.

January 15 2017

The thing is, it's not just that night.
It's that you made her feel so worthless that she,
Even knowing her worth,
Feels the loss of it all over again with every encounter in which a man is simply satisfied to call her beautiful
As if her body
Is all that is worth mentioning.
Every time she is touched
And her body remembers the past before it realizes that it is no longer a prisoner there
And so, she has died a thousand times by your hands
And you have never been anything more than a
tueur en série.
Serial killer.

January 15 2017

You've taught me many things for someone who never bothered to learn my name. That you can fit an entire night sky of darkness inside a soul, years of frozen winter within a heart.

January 16 2017

My bones are hollow and made of dust,
But they glitter in the sunlight
And this is all you see.

January 17 2017

And then two years later, two years from the darkest of nights, the winter midnight that had shattered her, the one out of which she had prayed for an escape, the one in which none had appeared; two years after this night, she had pulled it off. Her escape. Hers. She was gone, above the clouds and across an ocean and amongst the stars and away in a new place far from darkness, a new place where everything was beautiful.

January 18 2017

There are wolves in the world she whispered. And you know what else, what they never tell you? Winter lasts so much longer than a single season.

January 20 2017

The most amazing thing is that for you, it's just another day. And for me, it's the day you obliterated my entire world and the sun disappeared from the sky and I stopped believing in fairytales and my heart froze over until the ice couldn't grow any colder, until it shattered and broke apart. And you just call it Tuesday.

February 16 2017

It might not last forever, but neither do sunsets, and aren't they still beautiful? Aren't we?

February 23 2017

They say gambling is dangerous, I suppose we never cared.
We had a running bet against the universe:
That we could hold on to each other tighter
Than a fate destined to pull us apart

February 28 2017

And that's how it happens.
7 billion people on the planet and we're just strangers in a foreign city and then all of a sudden the Earth shifts and we're calling it love.

March 23 2017

And then all of a sudden, you're in your twenties, and you live in a strange and beautiful city in your own apartment, and you sleep in when you want to and stay up past midnight to dance on rooftops, and you remember when you were terrified you'd never escape that town, but this, it's nothing like you imagined. It's even better.

March 30 2017

I can always tell when I've dreamt of you.
Even when the memory disappears and evaporates into sleep vapors.
I awake cold
Even in spring
Even wrapped in blankets and someone else's arms.

April 27 2017

Disaster's where this is heading to
Longer pauses by the door
No one wants to say I love you
When leaving only leaves you wanting more
4am close your arms around me tighter
We've still got a little bit longer
Before it's a little bit lighter

April 29 2017

You can tell a lot about a person by looking at where they run away to.
For her it was art museums,
The ocean,
And you.

May 12 2017

Thinking about you makes me nauseous.
I have nightmares about running into you again. The kind that leave you terrified long after you're awake.
The thought of returning only reminds me why I left.
Why I fled thousands of miles and oceans and years away.
Why I love knowing my body is not on the same continent, not in the same hemisphere, the same time zone as yours. Nowhere close.
Nightmares about running into that smell of stale beer and sweat and agony and the way I can't forget eyes like that
Who knew empty was a color
Nightmares about whether you'll brush by me, a crowded street, whether I'll start shaking on a sidewalk, in a coffee shop, all of a sudden, the middle of a summer afternoon, if I'll freeze like I did then. Cold.
If you'll look at me a second longer than you should, if our eyes will cross, vague recognition, if you'll tell me I look familiar from somewhere, but you can't quite place me - It's so hard to remember girl's names you never knew,
Stolen memories that should never have belonged to you

May 15 2017

Wish we could freeze in that moment forever. The first time you called my name, the first time I turned around.

May 16 2017

She's sitting, legs dangling off the edge of the world, thinking how she's not ready to go back there, the place where she came from, how it's so horribly unfair because it's been dark for so long and only just now has she finally found the stars.

May 18 2017

It's a dangerous game you play
Getting addicted to those not made to stay.

May 19 2017

Lay next to me while infinity comes crashing down.

May 20 2017

I've been gone for so long, and I've gotten used to having an ocean between us. And you know what? I like it. Being outside of your time, in another dimension. Separate, apart, away. Gone. I like that you can't *touch me. I like that you can't even try. I like falling asleep on the other side of the world, under a different sky. I don't want to go back. I don't want to ever go back. Ever.*

June 1 2017 New York

Time runs out. Her year-long visa expires.

Paris, her other world, her armor, the love she had found, it is all stripped away. She has to go back to the place where she was murdered. Her heart is tearing out of her chest. She starts to feel cold again.

It is her birthday. She moves into a tiny apartment in the city where everything reminds her of the nothing town. Her bedroom does not have a door to close, let alone lock. She does not feel safe. No one understands why she is so upset. No one understands at all. She is no longer tucked away in another world across the ocean. Everything comes flooding back. She cries in her closet because it is the only place where she can shut the door, where no one will see her panic. Days and weeks and then months go by and she tries to settle in but nothing works. She is a stranger in her own city, a foreigner in her own country, in her own body.
She is drowning.
All she wants in the world is to go back to Paris.

July 8 2017

What would it be like if you had any idea of all the things you don't know about me?

July 12 2017

Insomnia: When your body and your heart sleep on different sides of the ocean.

July 17 2017

It amused her to no end, the way her reflection revealed absolutely nothing about her – and yet it was enough for them to believe they knew all of her secrets – or still more amusing, that she hadn't any secrets at all.

August 7 2017

Let's watch sand fall down in an hourglass,
Pray it doesn't bury us.

December 29th 2017 Paris

She has waited every moment of every day since the day she left to come back here. To this place, to the person that she is here – whole, happy – and to Him. She has waited every day since she left to finally tell Him that she loves Him. He sleeps with her, then tells her it is only her body he wanted.

She crumbles.

January 2018 New York

She is shattered, numb, broken. She flies back to New York in a blizzard and thinks that it makes sense that the world freeze over along with her heart. It makes sense that it be January. She thinks that she will never be worth anything more than her body to anyone. It is ironic, because to her, there is nothing more worthless. Ironic that it be the only thing anyone ever desire when it is the thing she despises the most. The thing that betrayed her. The thing that stayed numb, frozen, silent. Useless. She spirals into a serious depression and thinks that all she will ever be worth is sex. A hole for insertion. She feels invisible. Everyone believes she is simply upset over a breakup, a fling. She lets them.

January 6 2018

It's a boring story, I'm sure you've heard it a thousand times:

She falls in love, then she falls apart.

January 16 2018

She sometimes wondered if god had not overestimated her bones; that he had believed that a ribcage could be enough to protect her heart.

January 28 2018

He did this thing, she said, shaking her head at the memory, the way it still haunted her.
What?
He made me feel special. She whispered.

February 4 2018

People like to tell you that it's endlessly mysterious, the creation of worlds.
The way stars explode, the way they eventually fade to black.
They like to tell you that it's complicated, beyond understanding,
The idea that out of nothingness, atoms had collided at random and created something so complex and simple and radiant as the universe.
And that one day this universe would end, and these same atoms would disintegrate into dust and then nothingness again.

But she remembered you.

And how the two of you had collided at random and created a world together – complex and simple and radiant.

And then how one day that entire universe had exploded and collapsed, how now you and she were no longer anything more than strangers that happened to exist in the same orbit. And so, she understood how entire galaxies could be created and destroyed out of nothingness,

Because she still felt the remnants of your stardust between every aching beat of her heart.

February 13 2018

All of this is so horridly cliché. The way my heart threatens to tear itself out of my chest, the way I question whether it can continue to beat at all. What insult to injury, that in addition to the fact that I be in so much pain, that the pain must also be so thoroughly boring. There is nothing new to be said about this dull, dusty, aching thing. Heartbreak. Nothing interesting in this horror that has been written about a thousand times before, for so many centuries. And so, like always, I have said nothing. I have no words to explain the depth of my despair, this wound, how badly it stings. I have no words to explain that I am not simply upset over a boy, and no interest in platitudes that tell me not to worry, that there are so many more of him in some proverbial sea.

Not to worry, because I am beautiful.

My dog got hit by a car. I am jealous. Of its broken leg, the way it whimpers. Because this is visible and everyone seems more than capable of realizing that something is wrong, of offering it comfort. I have no idea how to explain that I feel just as much like I got hit by a car, and that I am just as much in need of comfort. I feel invisible.

It causes me physical pain to see couples together. It's not because of missing him. It's the knowledge, the realization that it is inaccessible to me. What they flaunt in front of me with their held hands and flowers: The kind of love that loves because of something more than desire. The kind of love that wants more than a body. A corpse. The kind of love that sees all of a person, and wants the whole chaotic, imperfect mess. Where all I am permitted is fragments. Scraps. I am wanted for my shell. I am wanted for a hole. A nothingness. Is this all that I am? A hole? A nothingness? Is this all that I am good for? All that I am worth? All that I will ever be? How could I have been such a fool, after everything, after everything! How could I, after all that has happened, after that night, how could I have still believed, even for an instant that someone would have, could have wanted more than that? And I wonder for the thousandth time since that night a thousand years ago in another winter, if he did something to make it that way. If I am stained, marked, poisoned, darkened, toxic. If I am forever barred from the kind of love that stays to hold you, that wants to wake up with you in the morning, the kind that does not discard you when it has finished, the kind that does not flee and disappear in the middle of the night. Perhaps some people are meant to be loved. And some only desired. It is only too obvious into which category I fall.

April 21 2018

What would it be to have the luxury of being one of the visible? The people whose problems surface. Those for whom dark moments do not remain in the shadows. The ones for whom tragedies slip off the tongue; or are worn on a sleeve. The one's whose hearts, even the deepest, darkest chambers, are seen and heard. Those who are able to be taken care of as a result. The visible.

What would it have been like to have had the liberty to fall apart? To openly break. What hedonistic extravagance, with what ease it would've been to do anything so simple, as to have shattered on the surface. What would I have done? So that anyone might have understood that I was in hell. Start failing all of my classes? Cut myself, get a million piercings, shave my head? Drop out of school? Turn to drugs?

These are things that people would've noticed. Red flags. Signs. Indications that there was a problem. Something was off. Something was wrong. Something must have instigated this change in behavior. Something must have happened. What happened? What's wrong? Are you okay? You seem different, are you alright? What happened? What happened? What happened?
Maybe they would've noticed. Maybe they would've asked questions. Maybe if they had asked the right ones, I could have told them. I could've broken.

But nobody noticed. Nobody noticed that I wasn't the same person. Nobody noticed a difference. Nobody noticed that I was murdered. Nobody noticed that my entire world changed overnight. Nobody noticed anything at all. I graduated Summa Cum Laude. I was pretty. A slight flicker, I moved to the other side of the world.

Teetering, steady, still.

No one batted an eye. It was pretty there too. Paradise. Pretty explains so much. It explains everything, if you let it.

Things like whether or not you're happy. Whether or not you have nightmares. Whether or not you have panic attacks that send you hyperventilating to the floor of the shower, wishing to swirl down the drain, to evaporate, to drown. But you don't. You don't drown. The drain is too small, and you are too entirely large, too entirely still there, this body that betrayed you, so you pick it up and put it to bed just as if it didn't.

To choose to break like that, wouldn't you, deep down, have to harbor the belief that someone was going to hear you? Wouldn't you have to be able to count on that? Why bother screaming if you know your cries are going to fall on deaf ears? No one would call 911 if we knew that there was no operator to pick up the phone. If you were already well aware that nobody was coming to save you. You wouldn't bother screaming. It is a waste of breath. Perhaps your last. A waste of oxygen, and a waste of time. People who know that no one will hear them don't waste their time screaming or waiting to be saved. It only takes that much more time away from them when they finally come to the realization that they are alone. And that no one is coming. That they are their only way out. That they must save themselves.

April 22 2018

A poem I wrote about a tree. (I was the tree):

I can no longer recall whether it was by frost or flame that I withered.
It's hard to remember the details.
And yet they are engrained in me.
Every branch, I think, must be evidence of my destruction. Evidence of the fire, or the blizzard, the scorching drought, the merciless winter that stripped me of so much life.
But I am still standing.
And this, in itself, renders the evidence of my destruction insufficient.
The very fact that I remain standing, remain to cast a shadow casts doubt on the severity of what did not manage to fell me.
It is not enough for you, just by staring at my limbs, to guess at the origins of my tragedy. To understand that something must have happened, that something must have made me this way.
That I wasn't always like this.
I was not born from an arid field.
It is with so much more conviction that we know there has been a storm, a lightning strike, when a tree is left cracked open, fractured, burnt, fallen.
But looking upon me now, it is easy to imagine that I have stood this way for centuries.
It is easy to imagine that there was no storm at all.

But they say if you cut me open, at my very core, my rings will tell my story.

The truth.

That just by counting the scars around my heart you'll be able to tell everything. What really happened. Guess at my age, my experiences, the hand of my murderer.

I wonder, if, when I am cut open before you, you will finally hear me in the emptiness. If you will hear the tale of an indigo night, caught too far from the safety of the forest, the night that I froze, or burned, alone in a waste land.

If you will wonder at the severity of the frost or flames that lay waste to the bed of flowers I grew from, if you will look upon the parched fields with newfound eyes, wonder at the strength of my silence, wonder at the fact that still, there are leaves clinging to my branches, that still, despite frost or flame,

I remain upright.

May 2018 Nice, South of France

She finishes her graduate degree, and once again, takes off to seek out the sun. The winter has been so hard and so long and she is trying desperately to trust someone else when he tells her that her body is not all that she is worth. She wants so badly to believe him. He wants to help her dust herself off and pick up the mess of broken pieces. She is so tired. So she lets him. He is in love with her the way that she is still in love with Him. She needs so badly for someone to love her without wanting her body. She needs him to be her friend. It is killing both of them to not be what the other wants.

She returns to New York, to reality, to the job that she took simply because she believes that one day, it might lead her back to Paris. She is trying so hard to be happy. She has a perfect new apartment, a stable job. But *one day* feels so far away.

June 30 2018 New York

I have wondered, for some time now, if I were to write it all down, all of it – what words would I use?

If ever I were to tell this story, of everything that happened this year, in between two continents and in two languages, the story of everything too that happened before, which made this year all the more tragic and beautiful and then cataclysmic and beautiful again – what could I possibly say? What could possibly be said? Are there any words sufficient in any of the languages I know to tell of the way a single heart might break and bend? To tell of two cities, two worlds, two universes? To tell of betrayals? To tell of a secret? What words to tell a story that has never been spoken aloud?

Do they exist at all?

And if they do, will they ever fall from my pen or tongue?

So much lost, so much changed, how does one write of a storm?

Simply by counting strikes of lightening?

What of the way the air carries all of the suspense and exhilaration of the next clap of thunder before ever it crashes against eardrums, the way the sky grows darker and darker slowly, so slowly one might not notice – and then, in an instant, all at once, everything is black.

What of hollowness- empty, frozen, numb, spiraling, cold.

What words for December, for the way I forgot how to breathe? All the waiting, the anticipation, the joy, the devastation, the destruction.

What words for January?

What of May? Soothing, warm, gentle.

What of love, disappearances, absences, people that go up in smoke.

What of my heart? The way it breaks in secret.

What of my body? The way it precludes my soul. The way it trembles at echoes and memories and braces itself to fall apart.

What of trauma? What words for healing? For memories, for One Day, for hope? What of me? What words for the shadows it seems I may never climb out of?

What words for everything that was said across an ocean?

What words to tell of being forced to plan for a job I am uninspired by; a future in a place that is on the other side of the world from everywhere I want to be.

August 27 2018

It's funny, that you could think touching my skin has anything at all to do with touching my heart.

September 13 2018

Am I really prepared for that? For you to know the truth in its entirety? How dark my world is on some days. How cold, how unforgiving. How much of a wasteland, how desolate, how numb my heart is? The nightmare that exists inside me.

Or more accurately, are you?

You say you cannot imagine, and you cannot. This is in part, my fault. I have never told you. Not like this. I did not think I would need to. I did not think some things required an explanation. I believed them to be self-evident. Believed that you could not help but understand. Rape. I thought that it was understood. That you would know what this meant.

I do not think you are prepared to know the reality. Can there be any other reason that you have refused thus far to see it? I have tried several times. To tell you that this world exists. The darkness inside of me that you do not believe in. That you refuse to see.

But this would be different. This would force you to know what I have lived. This is raw, this is intimate, this is graphic, unfiltered. And I wonder if it is too much, if it is unfair, if it is unkind to expose you to such a cruel place. If there is any real benefit to you knowing how much I have suffered; or if all it will do is make you suffer too.

But I have been screaming for so long, trapped within a sound-proofed room and it's like you have been deaf all this time, and it is so frustrating, so exhausting to carry this weight alone. I am so tired. Is it selfish? Is it vindictive? I want you to know what I have been through. I want you to know how I have suffered. I want you to know that I know what hell feels like, that I have lived it. That it exists inside of me. I want you to know that I am strong. I want you to know what I have lived through, what I have survived. On my own. Without your help. I want you to know that these words have been my only salvation, because I have been alone every day since that night. A prisoner of my own silence.

But is it of any use, really, to break that silence now?

September 19 2019

You hold tight to your mystery like it's the only thing keeping your head above water.

October 2018 Paris

She is going back to Paris, just for the weekend, because New York hurts. She is so unhappy there. She no longer knows how, no longer remembers what it is to be normal. She is so resentful of the callous nature of the world, resentful that no one know she is in pain, resentful that she cannot find the words to tell them.

Pretending is exhausting.

She has no one to talk to about what happened.

Hardly anyone knows anything happened at all. The people who do are all far away, have disappeared, or have seemingly forgotten. The friends she once had, before all the years she spent away across the ocean, they have moved on. She was gone for too long and she cut herself too completely off from the life she had had before. She is no longer the same person. The only time she feels like she is visible, where she can be entirely herself, is for 45 minutes, once a week inside the office of a therapist that no one knows she goes to see.

The plane takes off from JFK and she lets out a sigh of relief as the ground drops away. Escape.

They are sitting on the banks of the Seine; it is the first time she has seen him since he broke her heart nearly a year ago. They are talking and he is apologizing and explaining as if his life, as if his next breath depends on it, but she already knows she has forgiven him. She has never stopped loving him. It would be impossible. He is a part of her. They are broken in all of the same ways and she wants so badly for him to be the one. Sometimes, he lets her feel like he might be.

January 17 2019 New York

4 years. It has gone by in an instant and an eternity and I am so much the same and simultaneously forever altered. January 17 2015.
For the day to go by unrecognized feels wrong, disrespectful. I want to take into account what happened on this date, on that night, in that bed. To acknowledge the fact that a girl died there. Alone, in that apartment. True, another girl survived. But not the same one. I watched it happen. I saw what wasn't there in the mirror. My face. Gone.

And today, on this date, I am okay. More or less fine. Which is frustrating. I've gone through my normal routine. No one noticed anything being off. No one ever does. Not then, not now. But today is not a normal day. And I am askance at the idea that it too should pass unnoticed, silent, unimportant, unrecognized, unacknowledged. And caught up in the mundane normalcy of routine, of work, of dinner plans, I'm wondering when I get a chance. To grieve. For the girl that died. For me. For what happened. When do I get a second to acknowledge that today is not a normal day? Today is a black day, a dark day, one that I wish were stricken from the calendar.

The past few days have been odd. I know what's coming. I want to feel it. The full entirety of it. I think somehow that this will give me peace. To acknowledge, to feel the full extent of how wrong, of how devastating it all was. Is. But I feel nothing. More or less. Sometimes there are slight fissures, cracks, instances where for only a second, I sense the entire ocean of horror and tragedy that is inside me. But all that comes out is a drop. A heaving sob in the shower, hidden carefully amongst the sound of falling water, the kind of sob that wracks in your lungs, that pulls at your chest, hinting at all that is threatening to tear apart your heart. I'm left with a headache, without an appetite, and with the same numbing cold I felt then. I'm detached. Not entirely a part of this reality, because this nightmare I've continued to live in does not exist here. Or it does in the wavery forms that dreams can take after waking, not all together real, soon forgotten, discussed only in the short, awkward conversations that make it all too clear that nightmares are not a desirable topic of conversation for the light of day. That somehow it is too…much. Too disturbing. Too unavoidably dark. Too lacking in platitudes and silver linings. It is too unexplainable perhaps. It does not fit in. Not in the day light. Not even on this calendar date, the one day that I feel it deserves to fit into, that it deserves to have.

Today is much like that one. The other 17 of January. It is frigidly cold, gray. The trees are dead, branches hanging lifeless. The ground is frozen. The world is numb.
A thousand things are different and yet this is the same. Maybe the world knows. What today is. Whether or not it fits into reality, it's been all over my dreams. The past week or so, night after night, I've had nightmares violent to the point that I am disturbed my brain is capable of conjuring such ideas. Not necessarily of rape. Sometimes of other things. But in my dreams, I fight. I run. I scream. I am not frozen. I do not do nothing.

February 2019 Paris

She is crisscrossing the ocean on a chance that will finally allow her to go back to Paris for good. The day of her job interview she has the flu. He takes care of her and she thinks that there is something very wrong with the fact that she is happier with a 105-degree fever in Paris than she is on a daily basis in New York. She doesn't get the job. She knows she cannot stay in New York. It is impossible. Not when her heart is in Paris. She comes up with another plan.

June 2019 New York

She gets her visa to go back to France. Finally, she can go back to the place where she was happy, where she felt good. Where she was whole. She has waited two years for this. Things will be better again. She quits her job, moves out of her apartment. She is ready, happy to leave everything behind.

July 2019 Paris

She starts a new job and realizes that everything is different. She tries not to panic. Things will take time. She will adjust. Everything will be right again. Her worst fear is that what happened before will happen all over again. That she will be in love, in Paris, happy; and time will run out. Again. She doesn't know what to do to stop it from happening. She doesn't know how to make it turn out any differently this time. She feels helpless and is struggling not to feel hopeless as well. She hates hoping. Hoping and being continually disappointed. Because that night, in January, she had thought that someone would come. And no one came. And the hope that someone would have, well that was as bad as what happened. If not worse.

July 22 2019

Every part of me is in turbulence. I've been anxious, unsure, overwhelmed, nervous ever since arriving. I'm resisting the constant temptation to fall into a state of utter panic. I'm trying to tell myself that all of this is normal. That it will abate. I hope I have done the right thing. I can't help but wonder, in a confused, desperate way, what I'm doing here. Wonder at walking away from a secure job for a temporary one that I am overqualified for. Wonder at the real possibility of every truly being able to find permanent work here. At the real possibility of ever falling in love here or anywhere. At the real possibility of belonging to any particular place when I have lived across so many time zones without ever finding a permanent address, when I don't even feel at home in my own body. I'm second-guessing everything. I'm desperately clinging on to all that is familiar. But is that all that it is? Familiar? A last vestige of a year too perfect to last, a year that has all but entirely, so much like the now-spireless Notre Dame, gone up in smoke? I don't know if it's inevitable that I be bound once again for a broken heart. I don't know if it is at all avoidable. I can't take things continuing to disappear and fall apart. My heart is craving stable ground. My head is increasingly terrified that I will never find it in the things that I love.

October 2 2019

I hate the idea, that after all of this, you might have won. That I, thinking I had escaped, have never truly been able to outrun you. That any success I have had has been an illusion.

It's been nearly 5 years. I am 26. I feel increasingly that I am supposed to be doing what I love by now, be able to stand on my own, have found the one who will hold me forever. That I am supposed to be secure. Stable.

But I am in a temporary apartment in a temporary job, with temporary money, in love with a city that I do not know how to stay in, in love with a man who is only ever halfway there. I have no idea what happens next. I do not see a clear path forward. Every time, up until now, I have been able to come up with a plan. Somehow, I've convinced myself that I have been doing more than simply running away from you.

You, your hands, your breath on my neck.

I thought I had finally found something that was my own. Paris. Him. Happiness. But I do not know how to hold on to it. I feel my future slipping through my fingertips. I do not know what I want, simply what I do not. The degrees that I spent years and thousands of dollars earning do not inspire me. This in itself is devastating. The only thing I've ever truly been passionate about is writing and I do not know if anyone will ever read anything I have to say.

I see the rest of the world accelerating and I feel like I'm falling behind, and I don't know how to catch up. I feel frozen and maybe, for all the miles I have traveled, I haven't ever truly moved an inch since that night in January nearly 5 years ago.

And if it all comes crashing down now, is it just you, finally catching up with me? Was it delusional, to have ever really thought that I could have beaten you? That I could be successful, be happy, after you? Was it foolish to ever have thought that I could take off and leave you behind me?

You, your hands, your breath on my neck.

Was it only ever a fantasy, that no one would ever have to know that I had been broken, that no one would ever guess that there had been such darkness in my past for the way that I would shine so brightly?

They would be shocked. If at the end of this, I am at a loss. If I flounder. The ones who know me, but do not know of this. Of you. They would be shocked, if, finally, they see me drown. If I have to go back with no plan. No way out. But would it really be shocking? Or has it been inevitable all of this time. I am so tired. I do not know what to do. I feel so completely lost. Nothing feels like it is working. I hardly even know how to take care of myself. How to nourish this body. But is that a surprise, anything but inevitable? How could I be anything but lost after being forced on the run, a refugee from my own bones for nearly half a decade.

Is this the moment where I slow down, find clarity? Recharge? Catch my breath? Or is this the moment where my heart finally gives out?

October 12 2019

Searching for stability on a fault line. Everything is ephemeral. I'm dangerously attached to things that don't know how to do anything but disappear. What will become of me? What will become of me if everything falls apart again? When everything falls apart? Is there even any other possibility? Is there even one scenario in any alternate universe where this does not end in disaster?

October 27 2019

Love. Happiness. How excruciatingly simple. How tantalizingly unattainable. Or perhaps not.

March 15 2020

From the beginning of all of this, it has felt like the chaos devastating my heart was eerily aligned with the chaos devastating the world. I didn't know what it could mean. That my own universe felt as though it was crumbling; that everything in my heart be crashing down at the exact moment as the very same thing was taking place all across the world – governments, countries, coming to a standstill; a halt. Entire nations locked inside.
My heart, broken. Time, frozen.

As shocking as it all is; it is simultaneously utterly unsurprising. It makes sense. Simple, cosmic. How could it be any other way? Dreams die, and the world crumbles. My heart breaks and everything falls into madness. The universe is nothing but a reflection of the devastation of my soul. I told you I would love you forever, until the end of the world. And here we are.

The entire situation is so surreal that I am beginning to think that the two storms; the one wreaking havoc on my heart, and the one bringing the world to its knees; they must be linked. That it must all have some sort of divine purpose. And perhaps only in a situation as utterly bizarre and unprecedented as a pandemic; only as a result of a virus, a disease - could I truly have the opportunity to heal. Could I ever even hope to begin to mend my heart. Only in a quarantine, only with a month of obligated isolation, alone with the world on pause, could I ever hope to truly refocus on myself, on what I want, on where I'm going, on who I am, on what I deserve.

The entire world is currently experiencing the anxiety that I have been living with for months. Suddenly, everything is unknown for everyone. My anxiety about my job, my future, what it means for my home – suddenly all of these things are shared amongst millions of people all over the world.

I am still terrified at all of these things. All of these unknowns. So much so that taking any steps forward has been so anxiety provoking that it has been paralyzing. But, I have finally come to the point where I truly have nothing left to lose. My heart is shattered, like a mirror that has fallen, its glass splintered into a million fragments. Alone, accompanied by no one but time, I have no choice but to look at myself in the broken glass.

And put myself back together until the reflection is of someone that I am proud of. Someone I want to be.

Not one that I knew I wanted to tell; I also do not know how this story ends.

But the telling of it, perhaps that is more important than the ending. Perhaps that is what matters.

It is a dark tale, but aren't most? Even fairytales, the real ones, the original stories off of which our modern ones are based, they are filled with violence, devastation, tragedy.

And to truly tell a story of surviving, one must also tell a story of death. To tell of healing one must tell of being broken. To tell of hope one must tell first of despair. To tell of love, one must also know heartbreak. This story, this story without an end, this story that spans oceans and continents and languages, it tells of them all.

The girl I locked away, and all the words that were imprisoned along with her, she is not nice or pretty. But this is her story. Thank you for reading it. I think being seen will allow her to heal.

And I think, perhaps, the most likely reason that this story does not have an end is because it is not over.

                    Indeed, it is only just beginning.

Afterword

Why did I never say anything?

A thousand reasons. Anger, bitterness, resentment, denial, pride, fear.

It was difficult to imagine what was catastrophic for me being anything but a disaster for anyone else. I did not want to submit you to the hell I was in. I had not asked for it, it had been forced upon me. You had not asked for it, and I did not want to in turn, force it upon you. From the inside of my nightmare, it was inconceivable to me that you could know, that this horror could touch you, as insidious as it was, and not cause you immeasurable pain as well. I did not want to hurt you, for the simple fact that I was hurting. I did not see anything to be gained by dragging you along with me into suffering. I wanted to protect you; in the way I could not protect myself. This, still, is my greatest hesitation in telling you.

Shame. I was terrified that you would believe, like I so deeply feared, that it had been my fault. That I had done something wrong. That I should have, could have done something more to prevent it from happening. That it had been a failure on my part. That I was a failure. I was afraid that you would think that if I had been smarter, it never would have happened. That I had been an idiot. I also did not want you to ever have an image of me like that. For you to ever picture it, be able to see it, the loop that was on repeat in my head. My body like that. Broken. Naked. Pathetic. Him inside me. The whole thing, beyond the horror, was immeasurably, impossibly embarrassing. This is what happens, I guess, when the lines of a crime are blurred. Victim, perpetrator. I no longer could clearly tell the difference. I had already taken on the blame a thousand times; and could not take it if you blamed me as well. You cannot imagine all the ways I was hard on myself, detested myself, was disgusted at my reflection. It was difficult to imagine anyone looking at me any other way.

Shock. I, who had never been with a man, who had never had a boyfriend, who at just a few months shy of my 22 birthday, had never done anything more than kiss a few boys, who had grown jaded to always being wanted, who was waiting for someone that I would choose, that I wanted, who was waiting to feel something special, for someone special; was utterly horrified. I did not have the words to describe what had happened. I was so entirely numb that I could barely say anything at all. I did not want to talk about it. I did not want it to be real. It seemed so entirely unfair that in addition to the fact that I bear the burden of what happened, that I must also bear the burden of talking about the thing that was killing me. At the time, it was too much to bear. And then, as time went on, increasingly, I did not know how to explain all the weeks and months and then years that followed. I did not know if it was even possible, if there were even words that existed in any language at all that would be sufficient, so that you might understand. Simply saying the words "I was raped." was not enough. It did not tell the entire story. It did not really tell anything at all.

So this is it. The entire story, in the way I can best tell it.

Thank you for reading it.

Made in the USA
Columbia, SC
09 September 2021